*Front jacket:* A classic Victorian locomotive still hard at work in Pakistan. It is a passenger hauling inside-cylinder 4-4-0 with a driving wheel diameter of 6ft 2in.

*Front end paper:* The magnificent profile of a Pacific 4-6-2.

# STEAM TRAINS

*Above:* Firing is done manually on all but the largest engines and on a long run a fireman will shovel several tons of coal. Fortunately, the rule is little and often so brief periods of rest are possible. Considerable skills are required to coax the best from a steam locomotive and the crew work as a team.

*Overleaf:* Spinning wheels and flashing rods are one of the many alluring aspects of a steam engine in action. The valve gear in use here is Walschaerts, the standard system for most twentieth-century engines.

# STEAM TRAINS

## COLIN GARRATT

# Contents

*Left:* A typical American Mogul (2-6-0) working on the sugar plantations on the Philippine island of Negros. The engine is a hybrid, the tender having been taken from a different colored locomotive.

This book was devised and produced by Multimedia Publications (UK) Ltd

*Editor* **Richard Rosenfeld**
*Design* **Behram Kapadia**
*Picture research* **Jane Williams**
*Production* **Arnon Orbach**

Copyright © Multimedia Publications (UK) Ltd

ISBN 1-85106-001-4

A Kola Book

Originated by D S Colour International Ltd, London
Typeset by Rowland Phototypesetting (London) Ltd
Printed in Spain by Cayfosa, Barcelona
Dep. Legal B-30.098 - 1984

# Introduction

The world's first steam locomotive crawled from an ironworks in South Wales in 1804. It was a momentous historical event destined to change the face of Britain and much of the world. The steam railway enabled the industrial revolution to develop; at last raw materials and manufactured goods could be moved quickly and in bulk. Trade and industry mushroomed and the foundations of today's technological age were established.

## A thriving industry

Britain, the mother country of railways, built the first locomotives and, apart from constructing so many railways at home, was responsible for building and financing railways all over the world – partly because the British Empire covered such a vast area of the globe and partly because Britain was one of the world's leading traders. Other powerful countries with colonial interests followed Britain's example, notably America, Germany and France. They developed their own railway industries and eventually they, too, became exporters of locomotives and railway equipment.

As the network of railways grew throughout the world, countless different companies – either state-owned or private – came into existence. Each company had its own individual types of locomotives resulting in thousands of different classes being built. Apart from many individual designs, each major manufacturing country developed its own particular and different style of construction. At first these differences occurred only between Britain and America but by the turn of the century Germany, France, and Austria had developed characteristic engine designs.

## Overtaken by the roads

During the 1950s steam and the railways began to lose their popularity. Steam was being replaced by diesel and the railways were being pushed into second place by the roads – not least in Britain and America. The steam railway was a fast, safe, and energy-efficient industry. Its replacement by roads meant ugly freeways cutting through countryside, large numbers of accidents and a high consumption of oil reserves. Future generations will see this change as one of the more puzzling developments in twentieth-century transport.

The steam locomotive, which is easy to run and built to last, is still a useful form of transport, but it is put down as being old-fashioned by investment companies whose main interests are geared to producing rival forms of transport. Experts, however, have warned that the eventual shortage of oil will cause enormous problems. In such a climate it is unbelievable that steam trains and railways will continue to be ignored.

*Left:* A dramatic night shot of a veteran American engine working on Negros. Most of the island's engines are 60 years old so spare parts are difficult to obtain. Run-down engines are cannibalized for their good parts.

7

# The basic types

Almost a million steam locomotives were built throughout the world, but despite the enormous number of different kinds of design, most engines fall into six basic categories: industrial, main-line, passenger, freight, suburban and branch line and switching and mixed traffic.

Industrial engines are the workhorses of factory, colliery, plantation, or any other industry which needs to move around heavy materials. The engines are only used by the industry concerned and do not work on the main line networks, so are rarely seen by the public. Most industrials are smaller than main line engines, but there are some that are similar in size.

In contrast, the main-line passenger engine is a racehorse distinguished by large diameter driving wheels for fast running. Many express engines have a sleek appearance and those which hauled the fastest and most luxurious expresses were streamlined to reduce wind resistance. However, the freight haulers require a plodding strength to work mineral trains weighing up to 5000 tons. For such duties small wheels – often many of them – provide the necessary grip.

## Easy running

As the industrial revolution developed, sprawling suburbs grew around big cities so suburban engines were produced for working fast commuter trains. Tank engines fulfilled this purpose admirably as the absence of a tender – for carrying fuel – meant easy running in either direction. A close relation was the branch-line engine often built within a certain axle weight so it could run on light track.

Switching engines didn't appear until railway networks were widespread and huge interchange or shunting yards had evolved at important junctions. The standard switcher was rather like a large industrial – a tank engine with either six or eight driving wheels on which the locomotive's full weight rested to provide maximum grip.

Improvements in design and materials during the twentieth century meant engines with moderately sized wheels were able to undertake a wide range of main line duties so fewer different designs were needed. Known as mixed traffics these would have been used increasingly had steam development continued.

*Left:* This industrial was found at a large steelworks on India's eastern coalfield in Bengal. The engine is a heavy-duty tank with 18in diameter cylinders. It was built in England by Robert Stephenson & Hawthorn (RSH) in 1948.

*Left:* A British built 0-8-0 tank engine waits for the ladle to be filled with molten waste from the iron foundry at a Turkish steelworks. The engine is a typical industrial design and one of two specially built for the opening of the works in 1937. When the cauldrons are filled, they are tipped down the slag bank (*below left*). Performing the duty is an 0-6-0 saddle tank built by RSH during the 1940s to a basic design dating back to the early years of the century.

*Right:* Another RSH 0-6-0 saddle tank struggles to move a coal-train at a power station in the English Midlands. The slipping wheels cause sparks to fly from the track, while the steam makes the fire shoot shrouds of crimson embers skyward. *Below:* A power station in the South African Transvaal where these 4-8-2 tanks, built by North British of Glasgow, can be found. Though industrials, they are of main line proportions for the lines from South Africa's collieries to the national railway network are invariably lengthy and steeply graded.

*Left:* Note the old-time American styling on this meter-gauge Baldwin 2-8-0; high running plate, wooden cab with louvered windows, sand dome placed centrally on the boiler, and cylinders cast with smokebox saddle and protruding support stays. The engine was built in 1894 for Brazil's main-line Leopoldina Railway but has since been transferred to the sugar plantations for a further lease of active life. This is an interesting example of a main-line goods engine being transferred into industrial service.

*Left:* These 0-6-2 industrial side tanks are the standard shunting engines for the Calcutta Port Trust. They were built by Hunslet of Leeds, England, Henschel of Germany and Mitsubishi of Japan.

*Right:* This Baldwin 0-6-0 engine was originally built for sugar plantation service. It was exported from Philadelphia to Negros island in 1920. The huge cabbage-stack chimney is designed to suppress the emission of sparks. This particular engine is burning bagasse, the natural waste fiber of the sugar cane processing.

*Left:* Many German-built industrials are of the well tank type in which water is carried between the engine's frames. This contrasts with the normal practice of carrying water in saddle or side tanks. The engine is a 600 mm gauge 0-4-0 well tank working at a stone quarry in Uruguay. The oil (fuel) is carried in the barrel perched above the boiler.

*Right:* An approaching typhoon darkens the sky. The engine's crew are prepared for the onslaught and have put corrugated iron sheets around the tender to keep the bagasse dry. Their locomotive is an American Mogul built by Alco in 1921.

*Right:* Express passenger trains are still worked by steam in Poland. This handsome mechanically stoked Pt 47 Class 2-8-2 hauls a train from Krakow to the Czechoslovakian border.

*Below:* A fully streamlined Pacific (4-6-2) photographed in 1984 at Shenyang in northern China. The engine was one of 12 built in Japan for the South Manchurian Railway between 1934-5.

*Right:* A semi-streamlined Indian WP Pacific is prepared for the annual locomotive beauty competition held in New Delhi. The WPs are India's standard express passenger class – there are over 700 in service.

*Right:* A cross-country passenger train storms across the plains of the Pakistan Punjab headed by an inside-cylinder 4-4-0 – the principal form of express engine in Victorian England. Classified SPS by Pakistan Railways, these engines were first exported from Britain in 1904 and today, are still capable of spinning their 6ft 2in diameter driving wheels at speeds of 60 mph.

*Left:* One of the last British freight designs to survive in India is the XD Class 2-8-2 which dates back to the 1920s. The XDs are greatly revered and their crews maintain them in immaculate condition. Here one is seen at the head of a coal haul near Hyderabad.

*Below:* The big freeze-up which attacks northern China during the long winter is seen here in the famous coal-mining town of Fushun. The engine is one of the QJ Class heavy freight 2-10-2, some 4000 of which are currently in service, with more being built at Datong.

*Right:* A Chinese QJ Class 2-10-2 storms through temperatures of −4°F with a heavy freight from the steel town of Anshan to the port of Dalian on the Yellow Sea. The QJs are based on the Soviet LV Class. The design dates back to the late 1950s when Soviet technicians helped the Chinese to build their first locomotives.

*Below right:* A wintry scene on the arctic circle in northern Finland close to the Soviet border. Here is the last working survivor of the Finnish TV1 Class 2-8-0 heavy freight engine, 142 of which were built between 1917 and 1945. Most were built in Finland, but some came from Germany and Sweden. Finland also built TV1s for Latvia in exchange for linen.

*Left:* A 16 CR Class Pacific hastens away from Port Elizabeth, South Africa. These 1917-built engines reached speeds of 70 mph between stations only two miles apart.

*Below:* A fine roster of 14 American engines survives on the rural São João del Rei Rly in Brazil. The gauge is 2ft 6in. The oldest is dated 1889, the most recent 1912.

*Above left:* India's numerous branch lines embrace three gauges: 5ft 6in, meter and 2ft 6in. This 2ft 6in gauge Burdwan-Katwa system holds a British 0-6-4 branch tank of 1914. *Above right:* For operations on the light 5ft 6in gauge branches, the 0-4-2 tank was chosen.

*Below:* For the heaviest suburban and branch services on the 5ft 6in lines, Indian Railways introduced the WT Class 2-8-4 tank, built at Chittaranjan Works between 1959 and 1967.

*Above:* The standard British shunter was an 0-6-0 tank which evolved during the 1850s. This 1951 Sudanese example is one of the last in service. Another survivor in the shape of a saddle tank of 1904 (*below*) is still being used in Argentina.

*Above:* In China, an old JF Class 2-8-2 freight engine which has been relegated to shunting. America favored the saddle tank for lighter shunting duties. This Baldwin 0-6-2 switcher of the 1890s (*right*) remains in service at a Brazilian steelworks.

*Above:* The wild tsetse fly infested scrublands of Tanzania still resound to the wail of British locomotives. Here, on the line from Tabora to Mpanda, No. 2611, is a mixed traffic 2-8-2 Mikado exported from England.

*Left:* Paraguay's main line runs from the capital Asuncion to the Argentinian border 240 miles away. The railway uses the original mixed traffic Moguls exported from Scotland in 1910. In 1953 two further engines were supplied by the Yorkshire Engine Company.

*Above:* A British built steam crane lifts the bucket containing one ton of coal at Bandel depot in Bengal. Classified CWD, the 2-8-2 is a medium-range mixed traffic type supplied from America and Canada during World War II.

*Right:* The two main classes on Sudan railways are the 200 Class Pacific and 310 Class Mikado – the former for passenger, the latter for mixed traffic. They are similar in appearance. Here one of the 200 Class receives attention to its smokebox.

*Left:* One of the world's most remarkable steam survivors crosses a wooden trestle bridge built in the classic wild west style under American colonial rule. The engine is No.7, a four-cylinder Compound Mallet built in Philadelphia during the 1920s. It works on the Philippine island of Negros where many of the local inhabitants believe the engine to be haunted.

The Mallet's job is to convey mahogany logs from the mountain stands down to the coastal sawmill where, *below left*, the wagons are lined up by the equally remarkable Shay No.12. Decrepit in the extreme, the Mallet and Shay use the mahogany off-cuts as fuel.

*Right, top and bottom:* These 250 ton Mountain Class 4-8-2 and 2-8-4 Garratts worked the 332-mile line from Mombasa on the Indian Ocean, to the Kenyan capital Nairobi. Severe gradients are a challenge for the westbound trains as they climb the steep coastal escarpment for Nairobi lies over one mile above sea level. The Garratt was ideal for the job because of its powerful articulated design.

The Garratt's boiler is pivoted between two power units, one for water, the other for coal – an arrangement which provides a double-jointed engine whose boiler can be built to massive proportions.

# Fantastic Engines

Apart from development of the conventional locomotive, a whole tapestry of unusual designs evolved for specific purposes. Many were short-lived and exerted little or no influence, but others continue to play their specialized role. One of the oldest forms is the steam tram, an encased locomotive – with a steel housing around it – built to replace horses on city streets.

Even more fascinating is the fireless locomotive into which steam is injected from an external source – usually a factory. The fireless is ideal for shunting in factories which have a ready supply of high-pressure steam. When boiler pressure on the locomotive falls too low, it simply returns to the steam point for a recharge. Fireless engines have two distinct advantages: first, they are safe to use in industries where sparks from a conventional engine could wreak havoc – such as paper mills or armament factories – and second, they constitute a highly efficient low-cost shunter.

## 700 miles without water

Another type of engine with an unusual steam cycle is the condenser, built for working where water is unobtainable. After the steam has driven the pistons, it is condensed and pumped back into the tender, a system which enabled some condensers to run for 700 miles without taking water.

Some of the most interesting variations on the conventional engine are concerned with articulation to help the engine to maneuver more easily. This is vital where powerful engines are needed to work over routes which abound in sharp curves or have lightly laid track which demand the locomotive's weight to be spread over many axles.

The three best-known articulated engines are Mallets, Garratts and Shays. The Mallet colonized North America and in its ultimate form became one of the world's biggest steam locomotives, the Union Pacific's 520 ton Big Boy. In contrast the Garratt is associated with Africa, while the exotic Shay – originally the classic lumber engine of the American Pacific Northwest – appeared on lines used for transporting logs in various parts of the world.

*Left:* A boiler in an engine shed in Sudan. Boilers from withdrawn locomotives are occasionally used for other duties such as supplying steam for heating. *Inset:* Only a handful of steam trams survive. This fiery example, built by Borsig of Berlin in 1910, was found in the wilds of Paraguay.

*Above:* Fireless engines are an excellent low-cost choice for shunting work around factories which can provide a source of steam. When steam pressure falls the engine simply returns to the factory for a recharge. These Orenstein & Koppel fireless engines work at Ludlow Jute Mills, Calcutta.

*Above:* The principal articulated Mallet No. 7 and Shay No. 12.

*Above:* Another principal articulated is the Kitsom Meyer, the predecessor of the Garratt. The two sets of driving wheels are pivoted from the main frame and, although the firebox can be built to large proportions, the boiler is restricted in size.

*Above:* A boat has delivered raw jute to the jetty of the Ludlow mills where one of the company's fireless engines heads the consignment into the factory.

*Left:* This locomotive is the product of Sentinel, an English company. The engines were vertically boilered. Eight hundred and fifty examples were built at their Shrewsbury works between 1923 and 1957.

30

*Above:* The most celebrated condensing engines were the 90 25c Class 4-8-4s built in Scotland for working in South Africa's Karroo Desert. The engines were 100ft long, of which some 60ft was the tender where the condensing elements were situated.

*Right:* The Crane engine was another fascinating variation on the conventional locomotive and this Indian veteran is probably the only survivor on earth. In recent years Crane engines have been superseded by mobile diesel cranes and heavy-duty fork lift trucks.

# Into the 1990s

All over the world steam locomotives remain at work – the legacy of one and a half centuries when steam railway was the main means of land transport. The oldest examples are a pair of tender engines built in Manchester in 1873, but there are many survivors from around the turn of the century – particularly those from late Victorian and Edwardian Britain along with early exports from the "Big Three" American builders – Baldwin, Alco and Lima. Some of these remain as built, while others have had so many parts replaced that there is little of the original left.

Some 35 000 steam locomotives remain in service and at least 20 percent were built before 1930. In today's world, when so many things do not seem to be built to last, such statistics are a tribute to the pride of workmanship associated with the steam engine.

## Humble tasks

Most Western countries do not use steam power. The engines that remain are chiefly found in the Third World countries – especially those of Asia and Africa. China and India alone have at least half the world's steam survivors with China still building at a rate of some 300 engines a year.

Most of the world's remaining steam engines are confined to humble tasks, the more important duties, such as long-distance expresses, being in the hands of diesels or electrics. Gone are the days when steam engines were greyhounds capable of highballing passenger trains at speeds of almost two miles a minute. In China, however, new steam locomotives work long-distance mineral hauls weighing over 3000 tons.

Nowadays, steam is usually found on secondary lines, in shunting yards or amid industrial locations. But whether in the frozen wastes of Siberia, the wilds of Patagonia, the steaming Chaco of Paraguay, the deserts of Rajasthan, or the tropical balm of Cuba, the fires still burn, the whistles still blow, and the rhythms of man's most animated creation pulsate across the landscape. Fortunately, some will survive into the twenty-first century.

*Left:* Many enthusiasts regard Brazil's coal-carrying Teresa Cristina as one of the finest railways in the world. Operated entirely by steam, this meter-gauge network boasts powerful Texas type 2-10-4s capable of hauling loads of 1800 tons at 60 mph.

33

*Left:* Two brand new Chinese JS Class 2-8-2s undergoing a steam test at Datong. The JS was introduced in 1958 as a successor to the JF Class. It is used for secondary freight hauls, tripping and shunting duties.

*Below:* The erecting shop at Datong with JS Class 2-8-2s under construction. In the foreground is a combined cylinder block and smokebox saddle. The Chinese can produce a modern steam locomotive at one-seventh of the cost of an equivalent diesel and during 1984 two JSs were being built each day.

*Above:* In the castings shop at Datong a sand mold for the leading wheels of a JS Class is dried by jets of flaming coal gas, before being filled with molten metal from the furnace in the background. In the boiler shop (*above right*) a worker rivets the stays on a firebox.

*Right:* The driving wheels of a JS Class stand ready in the erecting shop. Once the engine in the background is completed, it will be taken to the steam test shed and within hours a fully fledged locomotive will have grown around these wheels.

*Left:* Having taken its refreshment, a Texas type 2-10-4 sidles away into the smoky haze.

*Above:* A stoker moves amid the gurgling giants to keep the fires topped up and boilers filled with water. *Below:* Sunlight filters through the blackened windows of a main-line depot in the South African Transvaal.

*Top:* In Chile's Atacama Desert the British built a
fabulous railway network, hundreds of miles long,
to convey nitrates and gold from the desert to ports
on the Pacific coast. The Kitson Meyer articulated
was the main source of motive power and here is
No.59, an 0-6-6-0 of 1907.

By the early years of the present century, American locomotives had become
tough and rugged; most had two cylinders and the more powerful engines
possessed massive fireboxes which spread out over the rear driving wheels.
Having equipped the home railways, America began looking for a vigorous export
market and their engines spread rapidly around the world. *Above:* An
American-inspired 4-8-2 in South Africa and, *right,* the Chinese VS class based on
the American JF.

*Left:* Transport old and new in Sudan as a 500 Class 4-8-2 rapidly overtakes the timeless plodding of a donkey cart.

*Right:* A British inside-cylinder 0-6-0 labors through hill country in the Pakistan Punjab. Similar engines ran the length and breadth of Britain for 125 years embracing hundreds of different classes. Today, these thoroughbreds can only be found on the Indian subcontinent.

*Below:* An Indian pig boy waters his herd in the lineside stream as "Cheetal" – a 2ft gauge well tank built by John Fowler of Leeds in 1923 to a German design – steams past with a train of sugar cane on the upper India mills system.

*Below right:* An Indian goat boy tends his flock alongside the Fort Gloster branch in Greater Calcutta. This line is worked by the last surviving HSM Class 2-8-0. The HSMs were classic British freight engines built for India's Bengal & Nagpur Railway between 1913-25.

*Overleaf:* A Javan sugar plantation during the five-month milling campaign. The 700mm gauge veteran on the left is "Wilis", an 0-4-2 tank built by Yung in 1901. On the right is "Smeroe", an 0-6-0 tender/tank exported by Orenstein & Koppel during the 1920s.

*Left:* Three o'clock in the morning at a remote plantation siding in Campos state, Brazil, as a beautifully styled 4-4-0 exported from Glasgow in 1892 waits for the cane wagons to be loaded.

*Right:* The locomotives of the Paraguayan Chaco burn wood and throw shrouds of crimson embers 100ft into the air. Trains don't need to whistle at night here as the constant display of fireworks can be seen a mile away. Paraguay's logging lines carry Quebracho wood from which tannin is obtained for making leather. Here is "Laurita", a 2ft 6in gauge 0-4-0 well tank built by Arthur Koppel of Berlin in 1898. An inscription proclaims her to be "the first locomotive on the Paraguayan Chaco."

*Below:* As the trains head southward from Harbin, they face a steep climb so most are double-headed. Often two QJs will be used, but on other occasions the pilot will be a JS, as shown here – the QJ behind being totally obscured by steam! All pilots detach after 60 miles and return "light" to Harbin to assist succeeding trains.

*Left:* Like fairground engines on display, a brace of colourfully painted Baldwins pause between duties at the Hawaii Philippine Company's sugar plantation on Negros.

Scenes like this would attract thousands of tourists in Britain, Europe, or America but, out in the Philippines where sugar is a vital export commodity, these engines represent hard dollars.

47

*Left:* Old Shay No.12 – built by Lima of Ohio in 1907 – flits through the jungle at the dead of night and sprays the tropical vegetation with fire. With a huge cylindrical chimney, circular off-pitch boiler, and wooden rectangular buffer beam, the Shay looks a weird beast, but in practice is ideal for working over rough tracks frequently engulfed in a muddy quagmire.

*Right:* Apart from Texas 2-10-4s, the Teresa Cristina line employs several smaller types such as this Baldwin 2-8-2 of 1946. Known as "Grimy Hog," it originally worked on Brazil's Centro Oeste network before being transferred to the Teresa Cristina. Hog is a classic American product, scaled down for meter-gauge track.

*Below:* A shapely American switcher built by Baldwins in November 1896 for Brazil's 5ft 6in gauge Paulista Railway. Upon withdrawal from service in 1944, the engine acquired a further lease of active life at a steelworks near São Paulo and today, 40 years later, it remains active amid the blazing furnaces.

*Left:* This S160 Class 2-8-0 was found lurking in a colliery yard at Fushun in China. The S160s are one of the most famous types in world history. They were designed by Major Marsh of the US Army for Britain, Europe and the Middle East during World War II. The Class totaled almost 2000 engines and all came from the "Big Three" American builders.

*Below:* The dependable QJ class working in temperatures of −18°F on the busy Peking main line in China.

# Decline and Fall

Why are steam locomotives declining? Many would say because they are old-fashioned, dirty, inefficient and uneconomic. But such remarks just reflect the mood of the day and often have little basis when the facts are analyzed. In truth, steam trains are out of fashion, not old-fashioned.

But oil interests dominate world commerce and politics so much so that it has been profitable to run down both steam engines and railways. Over the last 30 years tens of thousands of superb locomotives have been prematurely sent to breakers' yards or dumped into graveyards. A few countries have "mothballed" parts of their steam fleet in case of emergency, but most have annihilated them for their scrap value.

Locomotive graveyards are sad places where the once proud giants become reduced to rusting hulks. Some lie for years before eventually disappearing among the cacophony of the breakers' yard. The engines are pulled to pieces amid the noisy wrenching and tearing of metal and the distinctive stench of acetylene gas.

## Rescue and restoration

Fortunately, millions of people love the steam locomotive and refuse to allow it to become extinct. If it can't be saved on the main line it must be kept in working museums with a limited amount of running line, so that visitors can still enjoy a short journey by steam.

Railway preservation societies raise funds to purchase old branch lines, renovate derelict stations, re-lay tracks and rescue historic engines from scrapyards. Many preservationists spend most of their free time (and money) on the task so that steam trains will continue to be enjoyed by future generations.

Britain and America lead the world in railway preservation and in Britain alone over 60 working lines are in operation and almost 2 000 locomotives preserved. Such great achievements are a wonderful leisure and tourist attraction – a fitting tribute to the much-loved machines which served mankind faithfully for two centuries and, in so doing, changed the course of human history.

*Left:* The sad remains in an Indian scrapyard of XE Class 2-8-2 No.22520. This engine was exported by the legendary Clydeside shipbuilder William Beardmore in 1930 for the East Indian Railway. The XE Class totaled 93 engines delivered between 1928-45.

*Left:* The world's last giant Mallets on Java. American built, these 2-8-8-0s came from Alco in 1919.

*Below left:* One of the celebrated meter gauge McArthur Mikados of World War II lies dumped amid the mountains of the Greek Peloponnesus.

*Below:* Valve gear enmeshed by ever encroaching vegetation is a characteristic sight in the locomotive graveyard.

*Above:* The "Wreck of Tithorea" lies abandoned in a lonely coppice in Greece. The dead thistles and broken lamp heighten the grotesque atmosphere of this "haunted" locomotive.

*Above right:* A former Austrian Sudbahn 580 Class 2-10-0 lies abandoned in Greece. Wild flowers laced in purple add a note of sadness.

*Right:* A pair of French-styled 2-6-0 tanks from the meter gauge lines of the Greek Peloponnesus lie forgotten. Notice the abandoned shovel.

*Right:* Many historical Austrian engines lie abandoned in Greece as this graveyard scene reveals. The 580 Class in the foreground is complemented by five 80.9 Class 0-10-0s designed by the legendary Karl Golsdorf, Chief Mechanical Engineer of the Austrian State Railway from 1891-1916.

During his tenure of office, Golsdorf produced no less than 60 different locomotive designs. The 80.9s date back to 1900.

*Above:* Rejected as an outmoded form of technology, an unidentified and unsung workhorse lost amid the jungles of Brazil. Almost 3 000 of these 60 centimeter 0-8-0 tanks were built by 11 different German firms. After the Great War, the Feldbahns dispersed into industry – especially forestry railways – and some survived in Poland until 1983.

*Right:* The last of the celebrated Feldbahns, the German military engines of World War I. Almost 3000 of these 60 centimetre 0-8-0 tanks were built by 11 different German firms.

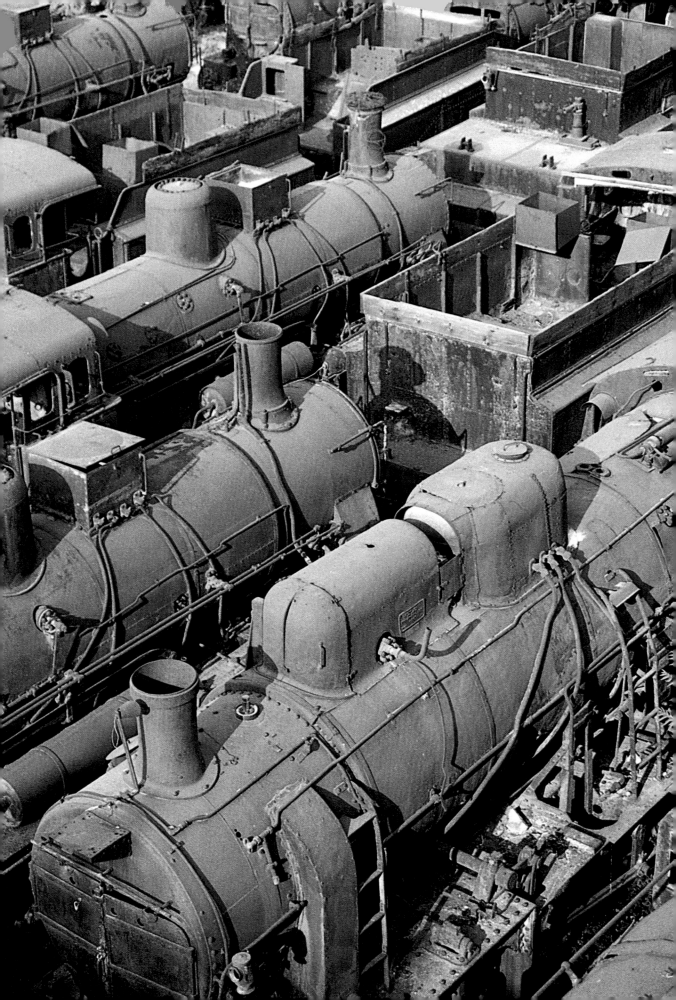

*Left:* British inside-cylinder 0-6-0s were the principal freight engines on the Indian sub-continent until the 1920s when they were superseded by larger 2-8-0s. In this scene at Sultanpur scrapyard, both types are seen being broken up.

*Left:* An Indian XE Class 2-8-2 being attacked with hammers by the demolition gangs. Twenty vicious back-breaking strokes are needed to remove one rivet head.

*Right:* This British 0-6-0 has its boiler cut open, revealing flue tubes caked white by scale.

*Above:* A typical builder's plate. The 14 inches by 20 inches refers to the engine's cylinder diameter and stroke; No.3741 signifies the number of engines built previously, while 1951 is the year of construction. Hunslet began building in 1864 and exported Britain's last steam locomotive in 1971.

*Top left:* More pieces of locomotive anatomy lie on the ground of the breakers' yard.

*Left:* Two of the famous "Black 5" Class 4-6-0s in the breakers' yard during the 1960s when the steam age in Britain ended. The Black 5s were a mixed traffic design with two outside cylinders and 6ft diameter driving wheels. The type first appeared in 1934 and, when building finished in 1951, a total of 842 were in service. Brilliant with express passenger and fast freight alike, the Black 5s have gone down in British locomotive history as one of the most outstanding designs ever produced.

*This page:* Three scenes from an Indian breakers yard. Every day of every week of every year, somewhere in the world, classic locomotives are being broken up. Many of the countries concerned have little feeling for their industrial past; they look only to the future and the new technology they believe to be superior. When all their locomotives are destroyed – and in some cases much of their railways too – there will be nothing left for future generations to see.

*Left:* Here is a reconstruction of Stephenson's "Rocket" of 1829. "Rocket" possessed several important features which became standard on all subsequent engines; a multi-tube boiler, direct drive from cylinders to wheels, and use of exhaust steam to create a vacuum to draw the fire.

*Below:* Many steam railwaymen feel a unity with their locomotives and a working relationship between man and machine. This unity is at the heart of much railway locomotion.

*Right:* A Brazilian scene showing the wheels of an old British-built engine being lovingly oiled.

*Right:* The mass closing of railways in Britain during the 1960s gave preservationists an opportunity to acquire sections of line. Invariably they chose branches in scenic areas in order to attract sufficient tourists to enable a service to be run.

To re-create the pride of the railway age, stations – as well as trains – had to be restored to their former glory and, after years of dedicated toil, derelict sites were transformed. This scene depicts Arley station on the 14-mile long Severn Valley Railway in the English Midlands.

Cold and inert, No.22.024, the last Yugoslavian State Railway 22
Class 2-6-2, stands at Varaždin in Croatia the day after being
withdrawn from service. Introduced in 1909, the 22s were a standard
Hungarian design, but after the splitting of the Austro-Hungarian
Empire following World War I – and the subsequent creation of
Yugoslavia – many 22s passed to the new country and some survived
into the 1980s. But sadly there was no preservation for No.22.024
because within a week she was due to go to nearby Zagreb for
breaking up.

## Picture Credits

*Rear jacket:* Yugoslavia still uses these fine looking 51 class 2-6-2
tanks on branch line service. The type originated in Hungary prior
to World War I.

*Rear endpaper:* A line-up of Japanese built locomotives at
Hsinchu depot in Taiwan. On the left is a 2-8-0 freight; in the
center a mixed traffic mogul and on the right a modern mixed
traffic 2-8-2.